WILLOW CRAFT
10 SIMPLE PROJECTS

JONATHAN RIDGEON

www.jonsbushcraft.com

CONTENTS

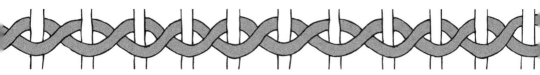

INTRODUCTION

The aim of this book is to show you how to make some of the most popular and inspiring willow craft projects other than baskets. There are items for both the home and garden, and all are great fun to make. You do not need any previous experience, the instructions have been designed to guide you every step of the way.

Although the projects are 'simple', you will find that they will still take practice and patience to make them well. Even something as simple as a star or heart may take a few attempts, so don't despair if you don't get things looking perfect first time.

The projects are ordered from easy to slightly more difficult, however you can feel free to start with any you like.

Have fun!

THE WILLOW

Willow from commercial growers

Most willow varieties cultivated for weaving have been specifically bred for the craft, resulting in superbly flexible material which can even be plaited or tied in knots. Willow growers will normally grow many different varieties; although usually one variety called Black Maul is favoured and accounts for the bulk of their crop.

After harvest, the willow is typically treated/ processed in some different ways, producing different types of weaving material. As a standard, most willow growers supply three different types: brown, buff and white:

Brown

'Brown' doesn't refer to the colour, it is the name given to willow which has been harvested then fully dried with its bark left un-stripped.

Buff

This is willow which has been boiled for a number of hours to loosen the bark which is then stripped off using a machine. The boiling process brings out the tannin in the bark (like tea) which dyes the stems an orangey brown colour.

White

This is willow which has had its bark stripped without being boiled first. The willow is harvested in winter before the buds sprout then stood in water to keep it alive. In the spring time when the sap rises, the bark will now strip off easily. A tool called a brake is used, which is essentially a pair of parallel prongs. The willow is inserted between and pulled through which strips the bark. This is a time consuming job which reflects in the price and availability.

> **Recommended willow suppliers in UK:**
> - Musgrove Willows
> - Coates English Willow
> - Somerset Willow Growers

Left to right: brown, buff, white.

Gathering and using wild willows

Not all willows are great for weaving; a number of wild varieties will break when bent to the necessary extremes. Osier (Salix Viminalis) is perhaps the most valued of the wild willows, its other common name being "Basket Willow". Various others will work well too and you don't even need to know their names. Simply give the stems a kink to gauge how flexible they are. Pick in the winter time when the leaves have fallen.

Less suitable willows can also be utilised in some projects where the bends do not need to be so extreme. The tension frame tray and wreath projects in this book are examples of this.

Hedgerows, marsh land, fen land and the banks of lakes and rivers are often good picking grounds. Hedgerows are particularly good as they tend to be cut back each year just like cultivated willow; this encourages the growth of nice straight shoots. (Remember to get permission from the land owner.)

3

Long willow shoots growing in a hedgerow.

Grow your own

Many willow suppliers sell fresh cuttings of the best varieties. These simply look like foot-long sections of thick willow, plant them out and they'll sprout roots and shoots. The harvest will be small for the first two or three years, but it's well worth the wait. This option gives you the satisfaction of cutting your own willow and seeing it through from plant to finished projects.

WILLOW PREPARATION

Soaking

Dried willows (brown, buff and white) need to be soaked before weaving, otherwise they'll snap. As a general guide, Brown willow needs to be in soak for one day per foot of length i.e. four foot willow is soaked for four days. The stripped willows (buff and white) take much less time: For material up to 5 foot long, soak for 1 ½ - 2 hours. For material 6 - 7 foot long soak for 2 – 4 hours.

You will need to completely submerge the willow in water; a tin bath or animal trough is useful for this. You can now also buy polythene 'soaking bags'. Avoid soaking more willow than you'll use. Willow can be dried off and then re-soaked; but it never looks quite as nice as the first time.

After soaking you can 'mellow' the willow, this is not strictly necessary, but is worthwhile. To do this, separate the willow out so the air can get around. It is then left for a short time so that just the surface water dries off (be careful, buff and white willow can dry quickly). The willow is now wrapped up in polythene or damp cloth and left over night. This time allows the moisture in the willow to evenly distribute. You'll now have some very nice material to work with.

Brown willow will stay workable for a few days; stripped material dries more quickly and will need re-soaking as necessary.

Working with green willow

'Green' means freshly cut. Due to its moisture content this material is flexible enough to work with as it is. However, you should bear in mind that willow shrinks quite significantly the first time it dries out. This means that a project woven with 'green' willow would look fine for a couple of weeks, but will become all loose later on. If you have harvested your own willow I would recommend working with it in a semi-dry state (See notes below), or dry it out completely and soak before use.

Working with semi-dry willow

'Green' willow can be left to dry out to a point where the shrinkage has taken place but it's still moist enough to weave without it snapping. Willow in this state is lovely to work with. Eventually it will dry completely and will be classed as 'brown' willow; this now needs to be soaked before being worked.

TOOLS

For this craft you need not spend a fortune on tools. In fact you may already have everything you need. For many of the projects in this book all you require is a pair of gardening secateurs/ snips, (A pair of sharp wire cutters would also work). Some of the projects also require the use of a sharp knife (e.g. pen knife/ gardening knife) and another tool called a bodkin. A bodkin is a bit like a screwdriver except with a point on the end, they can be bought from willow suppliers; or you can improvise. For most jobs a screwdriver would actually work, you could also get by with a six inch nail, a pointed hardwood stick or a chunky knitting needle.

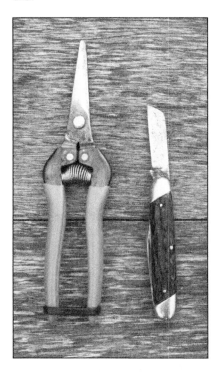

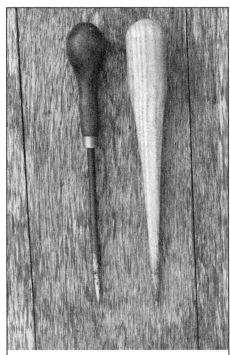

Two bodkins: A screwdriver filed to a point and another Whittled from Ash wood.

PROJECTS

1 Fish on a Rod

Cut a section of willow about 60cm (2 foot) long from the butt end of a rod which is not quite pencil thickness. Bend it at an angle in the middle as shown. This will be the nose end of the fish.

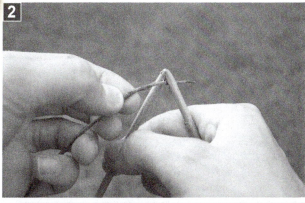

You'll need to use thinner willow for the weavers. Take a particularly slim rod to begin with. Starting with the thin end, position it into the apex of the 'triangle'. Now weave around each side in a figure of eight fashion. You will need to hold onto the tip to begin with so it stays in place.

4

Keep the sides of the fish angled out quite wide at this stage (almost 90 degrees) otherwise you'll end up with a very narrow fish. Also, place emphasis on bending the weaver around the sides in a smooth curve, rather than angled kinks.

5

When the weaver runs out, add a new one in as shown, so that it crosses the previous weaver. Hold it down tightly and continue weaving. Trim off the excess later.

6

The shape of the fish will soon have to stop getting wider and curve inwards towards the tail. Ease the rigid side rods over your thumb as shown to encourage the change in shape.

Now weave more tightly to bring the shape inward.

After more weaving, the side rods will cross. You'll need to pass the weaver between them to continue weaving.

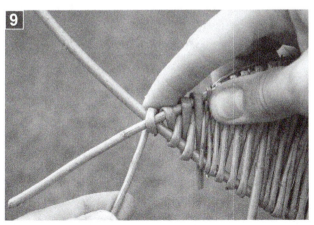

When the main body of the fish is woven, wrap the weaver around the point where the two sides cross. Then continue weaving as before on the other side.

Only a small amount of weaving is needed for the tail. Finish off by tucking the end under the last row. Pull tight.

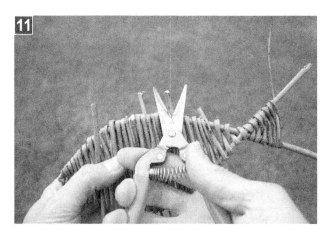

Trim off all the ends close to the edge.

I like to trim the tail ends to length with an outward facing point. Blunt ends may be more appropriate if this is for a child.

To attach the fish to a 'fishing rod', use a bodkin to open out a gap at the end.

Take the end of a fairly long rigid rod, thread it through the gap, loop it over and thread back through. Pull tight and loop back through again for a really tight hold. (If it broke, next time try twisting the willow to make the fibres more flexible).

2 Heart

Take one of the thin ends and use it to bind around and hold them in place. Use the same wrapping method as before.

Finally, cut off the thick ends to a point.

The method I use for making a star with even proportions is to pre-bend the willow in the right places, then it's just a case of making a series of moves, passing the willow under and over itself.

Surprisingly, to make a medium sized star with a hanging loop like the one in this tutorial you'll need to Start with a six foot willow rod.

Starting at the butt end make four sharp bends in the willow at equal intervals, In this example I went for a 16cm (6") spacing. You can cut a piece of willow to that length and use it as a measuring stick as shown.

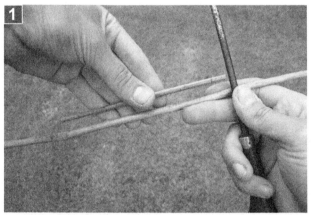

Bending thick willow to such a degree would normally cause it to snap, so send it tightly around a bodkin (or similar) which helps to prevent this.

Top tip: It's actually preferable if the section of willow before the first bend is about 2cm (3/4") longer, this helps to give room for tying off at the end.

Order of Weaving

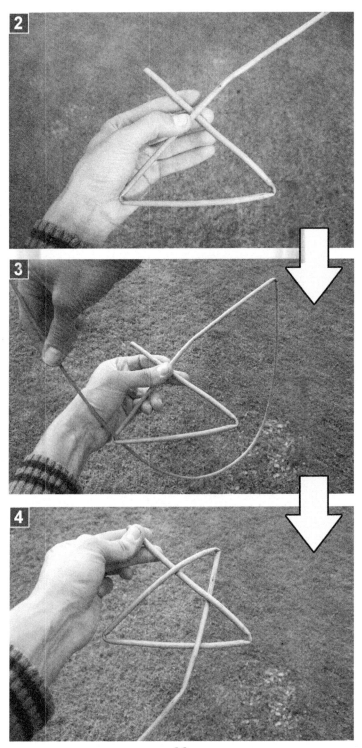

The last pass will require the willow to curve around quite severely as it is brought through. To avoid unwanted kinks, you'll first need to soften the willow a little. Do this by pulling the rod through your hand as shown. Notice how the willow is curved over the thumb in the direction it will be bending.

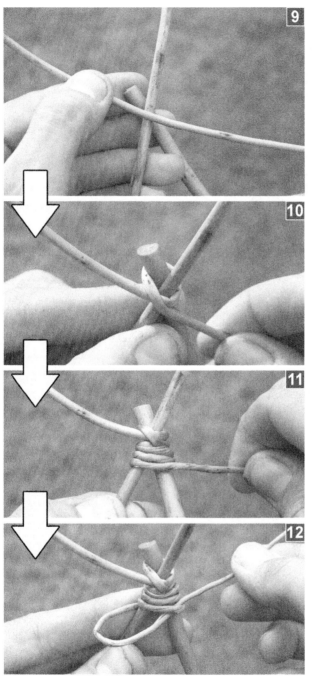

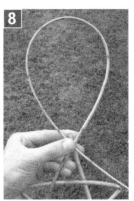

Loop the willow over and tie off as shown.

The tying is finished by passing the end under the last wrap and pulling tight. Trim the excess and you're done!

The tension frame tray is called so because it's the tension in the sticks which holds everything together. You start by making a hoop which is the 'frame'. It is worth noting that the larger the hoop, the less tension, meaning the weave will be loose. I tend to go for a diameter of about 9" (23cm) which works well. The hoop consists of four rods each about five foot long. Before we begin, each of these will need to be slightly softened, particularly at the thicker ends. Do this by pulling the willow through your hand as shown (Picture Above). Notice how the willow curves over the thumb.

Now take one of the rods, loop it around and pass the end through, similar to tying a standard overhand knot. Each end is then passed through once more as shown.

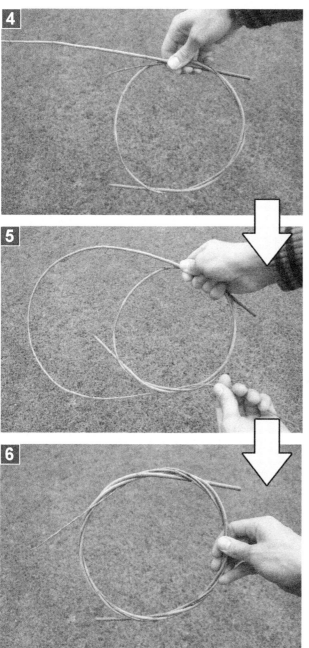

Position and hold the butt end of another rod into the hoop on the opposite side to the first butt. Notice how these ends point in oppo- site directions. They should also both be either on the back or the front.

Now pull the tip end through with your other hand.

Continue to wrap the tip end through and through again so that it gently spirals around.

Another two rods are added in as before so that all 4 butt ends are equally spaced. Any excess is then trimmed off. Notice how all the rods lay neatly alongside each other.

Five stout sticks are now placed on top of the hoop in the middle. Another rod is then taken up through the hoop, over these sticks and back down under again. This is the first 'tension stick'. Leaving a little spare, the excess is cut off.

More tension sticks are inserted so that they alternate under, over, under, over... as shown. For good tension Just use the thick ends of rods for now.

Working from the centre outwards, Continue to add in more sticks. As you get further towards completing, it is better and easier to insert thinner sticks.

Trim off excess from the centre rods, leaving an inch or so spare.

Finally, neatly trim off all the ends level with the outside of the hoop. Cutting them all at the same angle gives a nice finish.

The finished tray/ trivet.

Making the wreath ring is the same method as used in the tension frame tray project. Go to page 24, follow steps 1 - 7, Except you'll probably want to make this hoop slightly wider. Also it's preferable to use thicker and longer willow rods, and Rather than stopping after adding in just four rods, carry on until the hoop is much more bulky, this will probably take eight rods in all.

Now gather some sprigs of foliage, go for a walk and get inspired. My personal favourites tend to be Spruce, conifer, holly and ivy. I also look out for other special things such as cones, tree berries, and seed heads.

No string or wire is needed, simply shove the sprigs between the willow rods as shown. If you made a good hoop, the willow will be tight enough to firmly pinch the foliage in place.

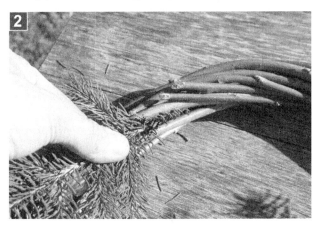

It is usually best to start with a base layer of greenery, such as spruce and conifer. Notice how I have arranged all the sprigs in the same direction, resulting in a nice flow of foliage.

The more eye-catching pieces can now be added in on top, such as the holly, ivy and other berries.

The finished wreath, front and back view.

Making the centre of the flower is the same method as used for making round basket bases. We begin by making a cross of sticks called a slath. The willow for this should be thicker than what you'll use for the weaving. Cut six lengths to about 20cm (8")long.

Three of the rods need to be split at their centres using a sharp bodkin or knife. The other three can then be inserted through the splits to form the cross.

Top tip: When assembling the cross, it's easiest to add the split rods onto a single normal rod first, then push the other two through.

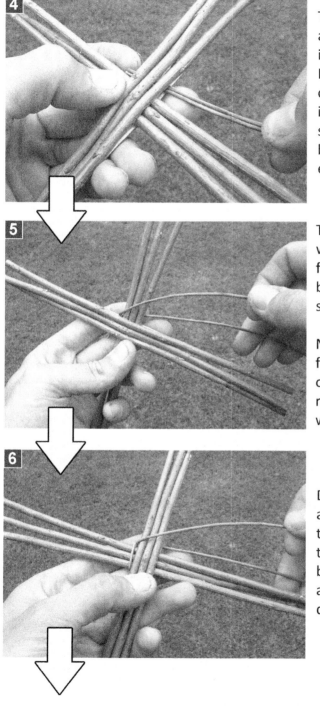

4

The weaving you are about to do is called 'pairing'. Insert the tip ends of two slim weavers into the slath as shown. We begin by weaving around each set of 3 rods.

5

To start, hold the weavers so that the first three rods are between them, as shown.

Now bring the weaver from the back up and over the next three rods, and the front weaver down behind.

6

Do the same again around the next three rods, bringing the weaver from the back up and over, and the front weaver down behind.

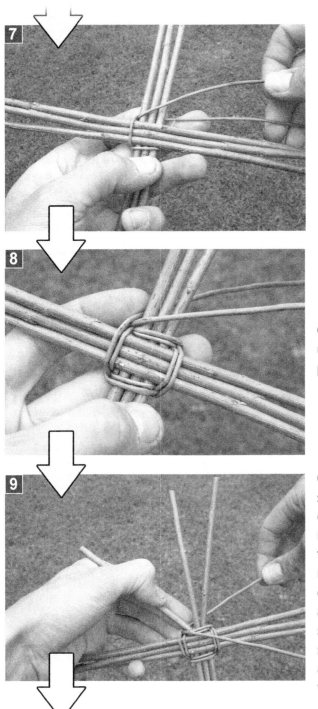

Continue around
until you have com-
pleted two rows.

Continue with the
same pairing weave,
except now you'll
need to weave be-
tween each individual
rod. Bend each set
of three rods open
as you come to them
so they'll become
spaced like spokes of
a wheel. Be firm, they
wont snap.

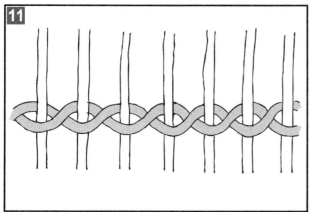

This diagram of a pairing weave woven around a series of stakes/ spokes should help in understanding how it should look.

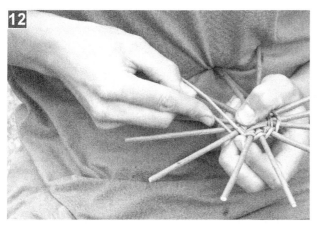

The key to getting a tight weave is to pull on the weavers firmly with every move.

Also, space the spokes evenly by moving and holding them in position while weaving around them.

Continue weaving around and around...

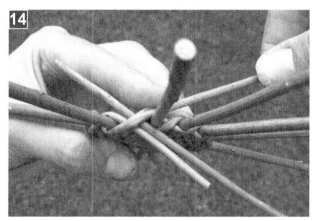

Splice in new weavers as shown, simply adding a new weaver alongside the old one and continuing... Trim the ends later.

In this example I have woven a disc of weave about 9cm (3 1/2") in diameter.

Finish off the ends by taking the weaver at the back and threading it under the previous row, as shown.

When trimming off the ends of weavers, ensure the stump still rests on a spoke.

You can now also, trim off the spokes a tiny bit out from the edge of the weave. If you made a good job of the weaving it won't unravel.

Time to add petals, six in all. Use fairly slim rods, point the butt ends of each so they are easier to insert.

Use a bodkin to ease open the weave a little next to a spoke, then insert one of the rods.

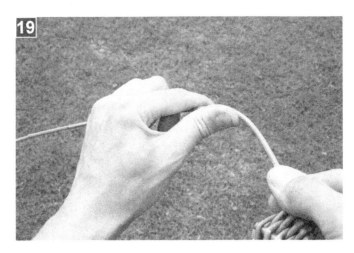

If you just loop the willow over into a petal shape it will likely kink. So to make it nicely rounded you'll first need to soften the willow. Do this by pulling the willow through your hand as shown. Notice how the willow curves over the thumb. Repeat a couple of times.

Loop the rod over and decide how big you'd like the petal to be. The tip end will be inserted three spokes around (one quarter of the way around). Snip the rod to length.

What you can now do is take the rod back out and use it as a measure to cut the other five to the same length.

If the woven disc was a clock face with each spoke being an hour, the but end of the first petal is inserted at 12 o'clock, and the tip end at 9 o'clock.

The ends of the next petal are inserted at 10 o'clock and 7 o'clock.

The next petal would span from 8 o'clock to 5 o'clock... Continue in this way until all six are in.

If you want pointed petals, give the willow rods a kink.

Add a flower stem by taking a stout rod of any suitable wood, point the end and insert it into the weave alongside a spoke. Job done!

7 Dragonfly

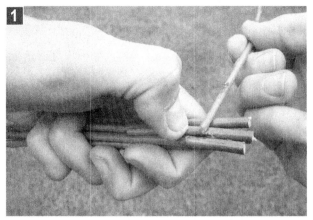

The dragonfly's body requires five slim four foot willow rods, plus another thin rod for binding these together to begin with.

Hold the five rods bunched together at the butt ends. Take the thin binder and firmly pinch it against these with the tip end pointing in the opposite direction. Bend it at 90 degrees a short distance from the end, as shown. Now wrap it around, going over the end you are pinching.

After wrapping around about five times, take the end and thread it under the last wrap. Pull very tight, then trim off the excess ends.

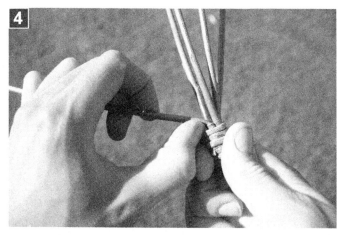

Give each rod a kink at its base just above the binding.

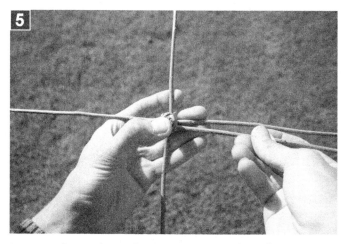

Then separate the rods so they are arranged as shown. Notice how two of the rods are paired up to start with (on the right). Also, the bound ends should be standing up in the centre.

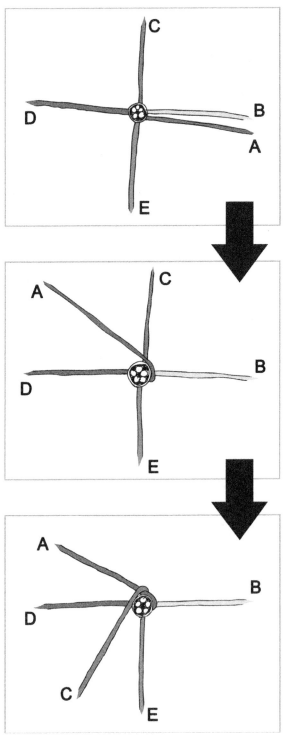

The weaving of the rods is the same method as used for making corn dollies. The first rod (A) is taken anti-clock-wise over two rods B & C. The last rod it passed (C) is the next rod to move, which now goes over two rods which will be A & D.

D would then be the next rod to move as it was the last one to be passed. It will go over C & E. The pattern goes on like this around and around...

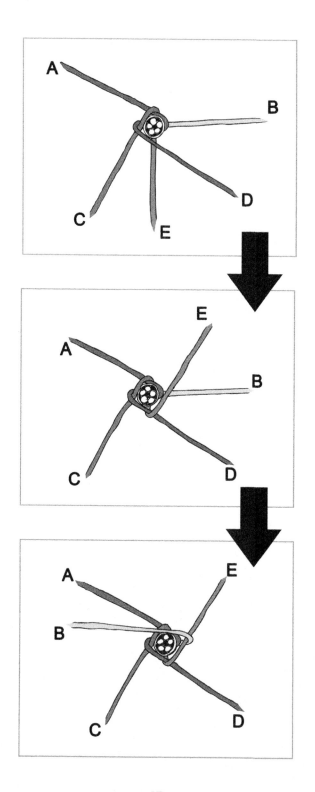

After some more weaving you will see a beautiful spiralled pattern emerge.

The body shape will naturally taper down thinner. When you are happy with the length, fold up four of the rods, bind around these using the other. Make six or seven wraps. Tie off by inserting the end under the last wrap, pull tightly and Snip off the excess. It can be nice to leave the four wispy ends trailing out the back.

Time to add wings. Dragonflies have two pairs of wings, We'll use a separate five foot willow rod for each. They are inserted through gaps in the body where appropriate.

Adding the first two wings: Point the ends of two rods. Shove them through the body, one from either direction. They should be a tight fit, but You may need to use a bodkin to open out the weave a little.

If you just loop the willow over into a wing shape it will likely kink. So to make them nicely rounded you'll first need to soften the willow. Do this by pulling the willow through your hand as shown. Notice how the willow curves over the thumb. Repeat a couple of times.

Loop the willow over and insert the tip through some gaps in the body next to the other end. Pull it through until you're happy with the size of the wing. To secure it, thread the end back through again (through an adjacent gap). Trim off the excess ends. That's one wing done, repeat for the other side.

The second pair of wings are inserted on top of the last pair in a slightly more forward position. The procedure is exactly the same as before.

A Dragonfly will look great as a garden ornament. You can attach it to the top of a willow stake and place it in a flower bed or planter.

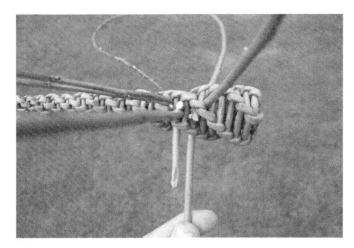

To do this, take a sturdy willow rod, cut the thin end off so you have a tip which is about pencil thickness. Push this up through the dragon-fly's body, bend it over and insert it back down again as pictured. Use a bodkin to open out the weave as necessary.

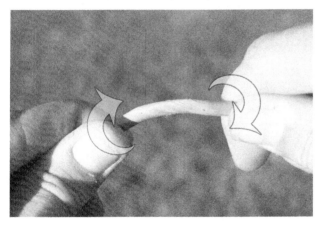

Note: Often, if you bend a thick rod over to such a degree it will snap. To prevent this, twist that section before-hand as shown.

8 Mouse

The bodies of these fun little mice are made in the same way as for the drag-onfly, except the body shape is not so long and needs to be-come more narrow from the middle to-wards the nose. Start by going to page 44, follow steps 1 - 7.

When the body is half done, begin to make the shape narrower in the following way:

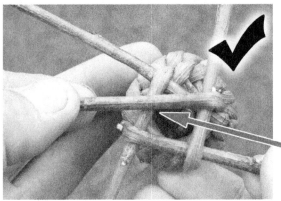

2
Each rod is taken over two others as usual, except, now you posi-tion the rods further down, about half way towards going over a third rod.

When the body has reached full length we need to bind the ends to-gether and cut off the excess. This is a great time to add in the mouse's whiskers too. For these, cut three very wispy ends from some buff willow (or similar).

Start by Folding up four of the rods, the remaining rod is used to bind around these.

Wrap around two or three times, then before making the last wrap, add in the whiskers between the rods. The last wrap it then made in front of the whiskers.

Tie off by inserting the end under the last wrap as shown, pull tightly. Cut off excess from the binder and the other four rods too.

For the mouse's legs, short lengths of willow can be inserted into the weave as shown. Point the ends of the sticks to make inserting them easier, using a bodkin can help too.

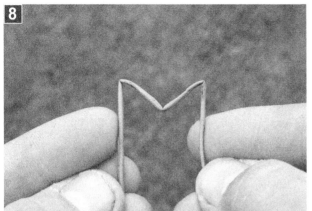

The ears can be fashioned from a small piece of willow bent into an 'M' shape. It is threaded through the body in a convenient place and then each end inserted into the weave as shown.

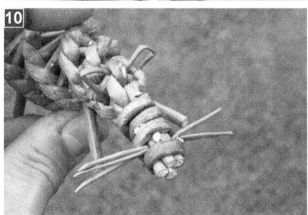

Finally, another piece can be inserted into the back
end for the tail.

That's the mouse complete :-)

⑨ Wooden Base Basket

As the name implies, with this type of basket we start with a wooden disc for our base. Plywood, hardboard, MDF or any other suitable board. Holes are drilled around the perimeter through which the uprights are inserted. After locking these off underneath, the sides are woven.

These baskets can be made for a variety of uses. In this tutorial I am making one to be used as a flower vase. A jam jar is placed inside to hold the water.

Making the base:
For this vase I used 9mm thick plywood. I marked out a circle 11cm in diameter, I then drew on a slightly smaller circle inside this to use as a guide for drilling the holes (about 8mm in from the edge). The spacing between holes shouldn't be too wide otherwise the weave on the sides will be loose. 12 holes seemed suitable in this case, I marked them out with equal spacing then drilled using a 5mm bit. (For reference, the spacing between my holes is approximately 2.8cm). Finally, cut the disc out using a coping saw, electric jigsaw or similar. Afterwards, you may also want to sand the edges.

Straight willow rods are now inserted through the
holes leaving a finger's length sticking out underneath
as shown. Tie the tip ends together for now.

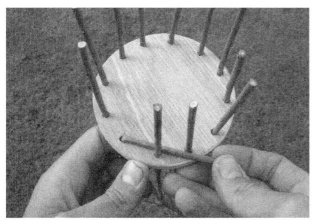

Stage 2

To lock the rods off underneath, take one rod down to the right behind its neighbour with the end resting up on the outside. Then, In the same way, take the next rod (to the right) down behind the next rod. Continue in this way all the way around. The last rod will need tucking under the first to complete the pattern. The ends are trimmed level with the edge of the base.

We can now begin working on the sides. The willow used for weaving should all be a little thinner than the uprights. It's best to start with a band of weave called a Wale. There are a few variations of this but we'll keep it simple and do a 'three rod wale'.

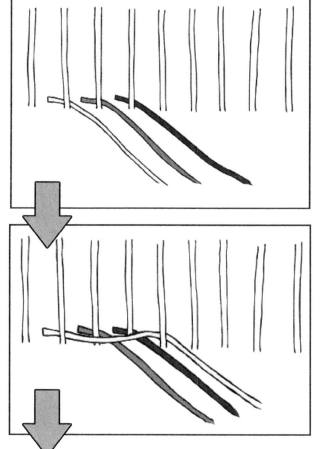

Begin by placing the but ends of 3 rods behind 3 consecutive stakes as shown.

Now take the left-most weaver in front of two uprights, behind the next and out to the front, as shown.

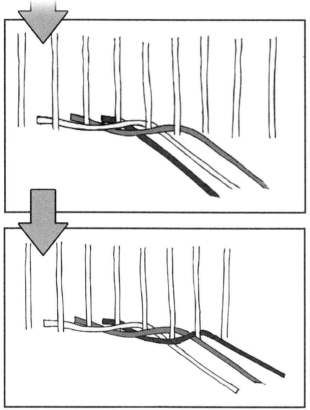

Now take the next leftmost weaver and weave it in the same way: In front of two uprights, behind the next and out to the front.

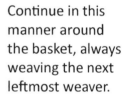

Continue in this manner around the basket, always weaving the next leftmost weaver.

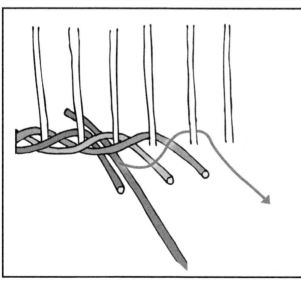

You can weave one or two rows, it's up to you. If weaving two rows the willow will likely run out or get too thin before you finish. Add new weavers in one by one when necessary. The butt end of the new weaver is simply inserted alongside the old weaver as shown.

To complete the wale, carry on until the weavers are directly above the ends from the beginning, then stop and cut off the excess.

Trim off all the ends half way between the uprights as shown.

You can now move on to the main weave for the sides. If you have an odd number of uprights you can simply do a plain weave using one weaver. Add the butt end in behind an upright, then weave it in-out-in-out around the basket...

If like in this example you have an even amount of uprights, you will need to work with two weavers, one 'chasing' the other. Start one weaver off, weaving it in and out for a few moves, then add in another one place behind the butt end of the first. Switch between weaving one weaver a little and then the other. It is important that one does not overtake the other at any point.

Note: After a little more weaving, untie the uprights at the top, other-wise the shape of the basket may start to go inwards.

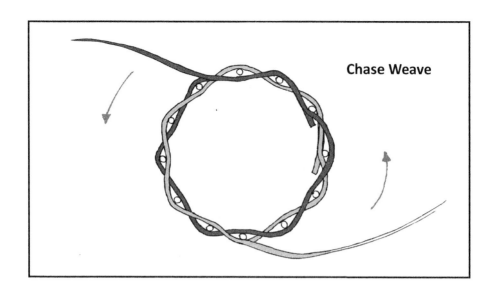

Chase Weave

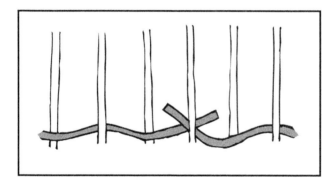

When weavers run out, splice in new ones as shown. Match the thickness of the ends; adding thick ends to thick and thin to thin.

Sometimes the width of the basket can start to get narrower. If you notice this happening, hold each upright outwards a little while you weave around them. This will get the shape back on track.

Press the weave down as you go. When you're happy with the height, stop and weave a layer of wale on top.

Remember how we locked off the uprights at the very beginning... Use the same technique for finishing off the top.

When trimming off the ends be careful not to cut them too short otherwise they'll not lock down. Each end should rest on the outside against an upright. The basket is now complete!

10 Fat Ball Bird Feeder

For this project a board with a circle of holes drilled through is used to hold the vertical rods in position while weaving. Later on, the nearly complete feeder is separated from the board and finished off.

In this example I marked out a circle 8.5cm (3 1/4") in diameter onto an off-cut of plywood. 16 holes were appropriate for this size; I marked them out with equal spacing and drilled with a 6mm bit.

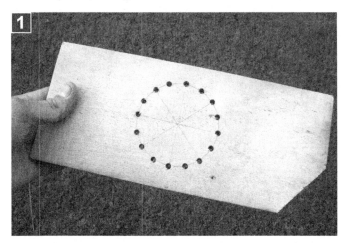

Insert willow rods through the holes. There needs to be about a finger's length of material poking out the other side as shown. Tie the rods together at their tip ends too.

It's good to begin with a border of weave called a three rod wale. This will help to firm-up the uprights and looks nice too. On the finished feeder this will be the layer under the rim. It's convenient to weave with the board on your lap as shown.

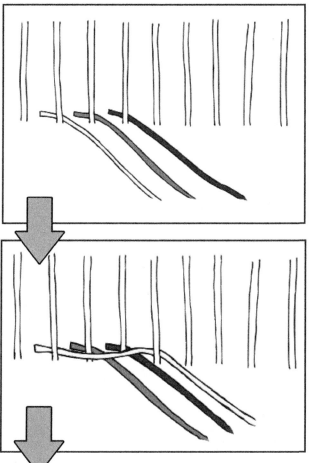

Begin by Placing the but ends of 3 rods behind 3 consecutive stakes as shown. Use rods which are a little thinner than the stakes.

Now take the left-most weaver in front of two stakes, behind the next and out to the front, as shown.

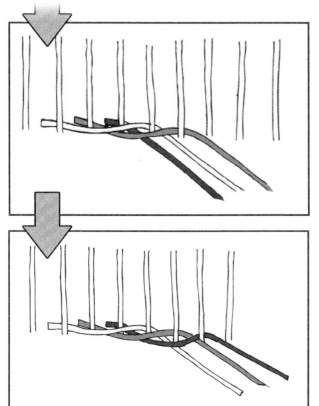

Now take the next leftmost weaver and weave it in the same way: In front of two stakes, behind the next and out to the front.

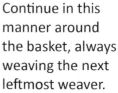

Continue in this manner around the basket, always weaving the next leftmost weaver.

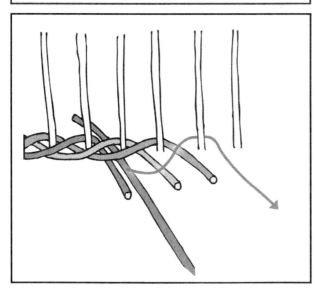

You can weave one or two rows, it's up to you. If weaving two rows the willow may run out or get too thin before you finish. Add new weavers in one by one when necessary. The butt end of the new weaver is simply inserted alongside the old weaver as shown.

To complete the wale, carry on until the weavers are directly above the ends from the beginning, then stop and cut off the excess.

Stage 4

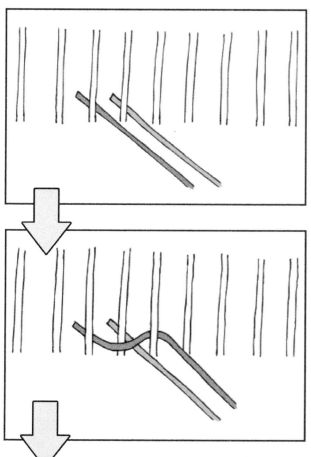

On top of the wale, we now begin a new technique called pairing. This is similar to a wale, except we only use two weavers.

Begin by placing the butt ends of two weavers behind two stakes as shown. Use weavers which are a little thinner than the stakes.

Now take the left-hand weaver in front of one stake, behind the next and out to the front, As shown.

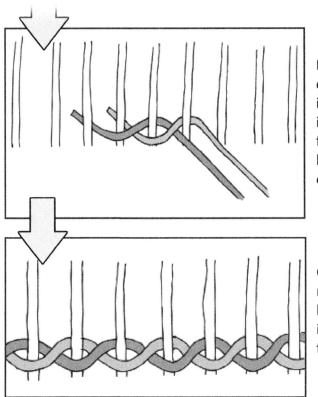

Now weave the other weaver (which is now on the left) in the same way: in front of one stake, behind the next and out to the front.

Continue in this manner around the basket, always taking the next weaver from the left.

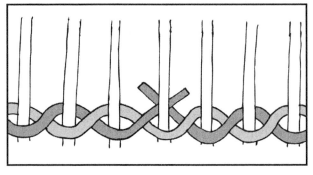

When weavers come to an end, add new ones in as shown, so that the ends cross behind a stake. Add butt ends to butt ends and tip ends to tip ends.

Weave around until you have a layer of weave one or two inches thick. Then continue with the same technique except start inclining at an angle so that the weave begins to spiral its way up the stakes as shown.

Note: So that you don't have to join in new weavers during the spiralling, join in two long weavers beforehand.

You need to continue weaving, bringing the shape in narrower until all the uprights come together. Plan how big you want the inside to be by temporarily putting the fat balls inside. This feeder will hold four.

Stage 7

After weaving along to the desired length, the two tip ends are held up and bound in together with the uprights.

For the binder use another thin rod, pinch the butt end in place parallel with the other rods. Then bend it at 90 degrees a short distance from the end, as shown. Now wrap it around, going over the end you are pinching.

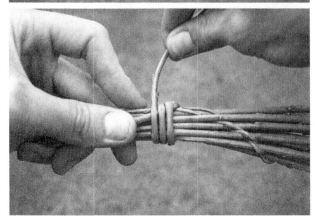

After about five wraps take the end and thread it under the last wrap. Pull very tight, then trim off the excess.

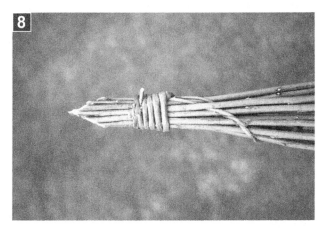

Trim off all the rods.

Remove the board.

The stakes need to be locked off on top. Here is a very simple method:

Take one rod down to the right behind its neighbour with the end resting up on the outside. Then, In the same way, take the next rod (to the right) down behind the next rod. Continue in this way all the way around. The last rod will need tucking under the first to complete the pattern.

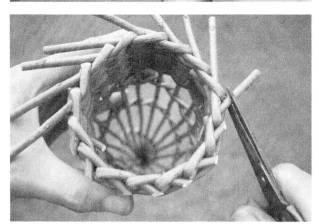

The ends can now be trimmed off. When doing so, be careful not to cut them too short. Each end should rest on the outside against an upright.

Now all we have to do is add a hanging loop. This is made from two rods, point their ends to make inserting them easier. Start by pushing one in alongside an upright. Open the weave out a little using a bodkin if needed.

Now arch the rod over and insert the tip end through the weave on the opposite side under the wale. Pull it through until you're happy with the size.

Now wrap the end around the loop back to the other side, as shown.

The second rod is now inserted on the opposite side to the first, then wrapped around the loop. The tip end is inserted under the wale as before, then wrapped back again.

Notice how all the wrapping is done in the same way so that the rods lie next to each other resembling a rope.

To secure the tip ends, simply insert them back through the weave to the inside and cut off the excess. That's the feeder finished!

Printed in Great Britain
by Amazon